THE **SECRETS** OF TOLKIEN'S WORLD

THE PEOPLES AND PLACES OF MIDDLE-EARTH

ᚾᚪᛁᚷᛒᛗᛗᚱᚷᚾᛋᚳᛁᛁᛚᚷᛈᚾᚪᛏᛁᛚᚱᚷᚷᛗ

GARETH HANRAHAN

With illustrations by
PETER MCKINSTRY

CARLTON
KIDS

CONTENTS

INTRODUCTION

The Red Book is one of the great mysteries of antiquity. Several versions can be found in libraries and museums around the world, all copied from a much older book. Written in strange scripts, the Red Book couldn't be understood until a professor, expert in ancient languages, discovered the key to unlocking its secrets.

Among the riches he revealed, were the myths and legends of a place known as Middle-earth. These include two long accounts written by Bilbo and Frodo Baggins, a scholar and his nephew from a previously unknown people called Hobbits.

The Red Book is not a single story or history. It collects together many different texts, including stories of great quests, myths, tales, family histories, maps and even poetry. Together, these reveal Middle-earth as a land of magic, where elves walked in the forests and dragons slumbered in dark caves.

Whether Middle-earth was a previous age of our own world is not clear. If we believe the Red Book, we live in the long-foretold age of Men that followed the Elder Days and the Middle Days.

Some experts believe that the Red Book is the history of an unknown age of our world. Others consider it to be the work of an imaginative professor, who gave us a glimpse of another world and time, through tales of astounding beauty and power. *Tolkien's World* independently explores J.R.R. Tolkien's work to reveal the magical world of Middle-earth.

THE FREE PEOPLES

The Free Peoples was the name given to the races who fought against the enslavement of all the living things in Middle-earth by the Enemy.

The Elves were the first of the Free Peoples to awaken, long ago on the shore of a lake under the first stars. The tribes of the Firstborn wandered for many years. Some stayed in the forests of Middle-earth, while others sailed across the sea to the Undying Lands.

Next came the Dwarves and Ents, born out of stone and wood respectively. Both were created by the Valar, the divine powers set to watch over Middle-earth. The Dwarves lived in the mountains, while the Ents tended the wild woods.

The first Men awoke with the rising of the sun. Men were short-lived and more numerous than the other races. Some mistrusted the Elves, but others learned from them. From the union of Elves and Men came the Half-elven, of whom much is told in the Red Book.

No great tales, however, are told of the origins of Hobbits. Perhaps they were related to Men, but grew away from their kin, becoming smaller and cleverer, until they could slip out of sight in a way that seemed magical.

HOBBITS

Hobbits were peaceful folk who lived in the countryside of the Shire. They farmed the land and were largely forgotten by the wider world. It was only towards the end of the Third Age that Hobbits played a part in the great history of Middle-earth.

Happy Halflings

Hobbits were half the height of Men, so they were sometimes known as Halflings. They were plump and cheerful, with thick curly hair and hairy feet. Hobbits didn't wear shoes and could move about almost silently.

Hobbits lived quiet, uneventful lives and enjoyed simple things, such as good food, music and parties. They were peace-loving, but could be brave and fierce. A few notable hobbits even had great adventures.

The Shire

The Shire lay in the north of Middle-earth. It was once part of the North Kingdom of Arnor and was originally given to the Hobbits by King Argeleb II. However, by the close of the Third Age, Arnor was long gone and only a few scholarly hobbits remembered their ancient history.

Hobbits lived in hobbit holes with round doors and windows built into the hillsides.

BILBO BAGGINS

Hobbits were quiet people and not the sort to go around having adventures. So it was a surprise when Bilbo Baggins, a respectable gentlehobbit, left his comfortable hobbit hole at Bag End and set off on a quest with a wizard and a strange band of dwarves.

Family History

Bilbo's father was Bungo Baggins, a wealthy hobbit from Hobbiton, but his mother, Belladonna, was from the more eccentric Took family. Bilbo probably got his adventurous side from her. Many great hobbits had Tooks in their family tree, such as the great 'Bullroarer' Took, who went down in Hobbit history for killing a goblin chief at the Battle of Greenfields.

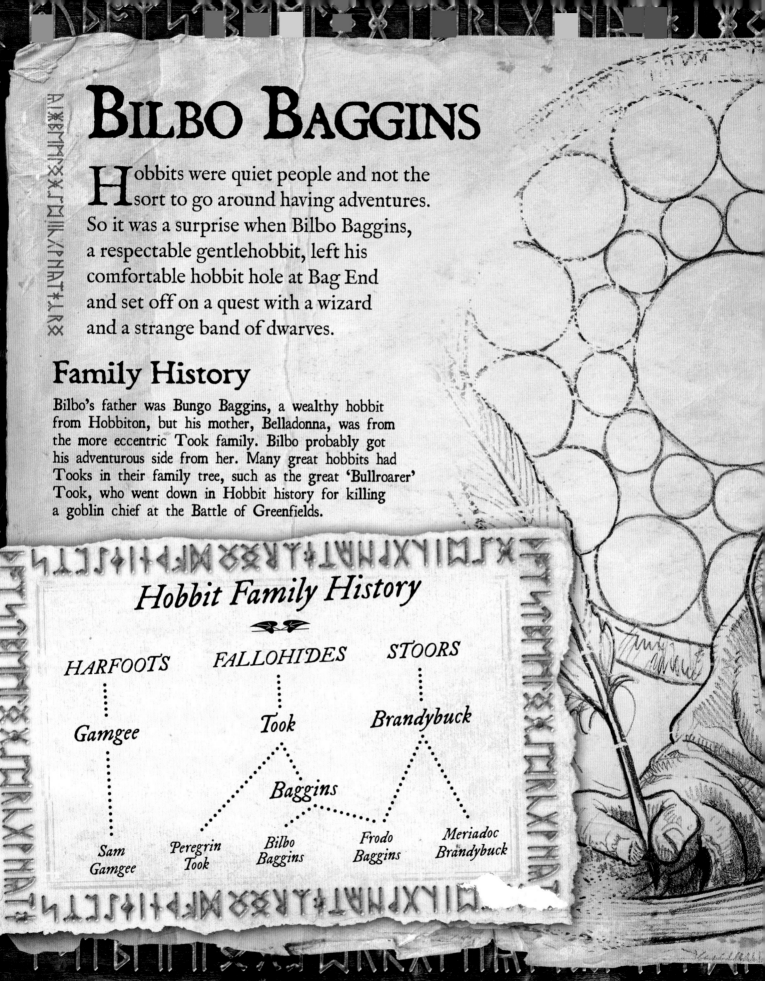

Hobbit Family History

HARFOOTS   FALLOHIDES   STOORS

Gamgee   Took   Brandybuck

                        Baggins

Sam   Peregrin   Bilbo   Frodo   Meriadoc
Gamgee   Took   Baggins   Baggins   Brandybuck

After his adventures, Bilbo wrote about his part in what became known as the Quest of Erebor.

Bilbo the Burglar

Only the wizard Gandalf studied the ways of Hobbits. He knew them better than they knew themselves, so he saw that Bilbo had a hidden adventurous streak. When Thorin's company needed a burglar to sneak into a dragon's lair, Gandalf knew that Bilbo was perfect for the job. He put a secret mark on Bilbo's front door and arranged for Thorin and the dwarves to meet him there.

The One Ring

During his adventures, Bilbo found a magical gold ring that could make its wearer invisible. He did not know it, but this was the One Ring, the most powerful object in all Middle-earth. Anyone who carried it was tempted to use its power. Only a hobbit could resist its evil for long.

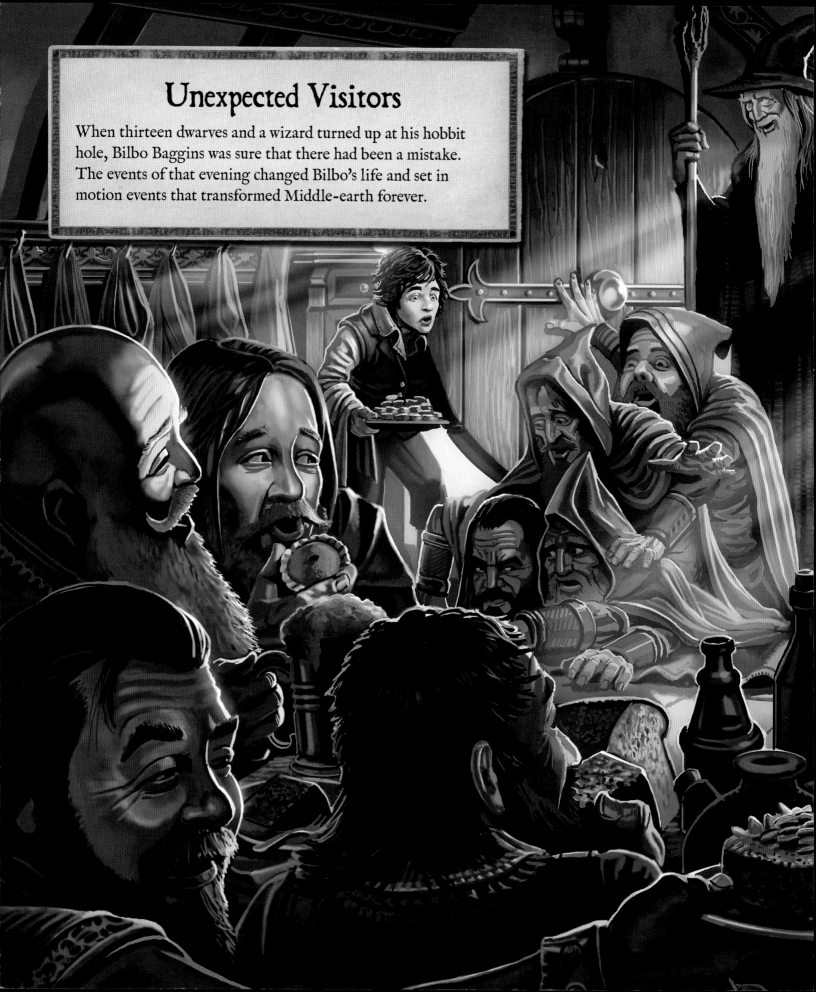

Unexpected Visitors

When thirteen dwarves and a wizard turned up at his hobbit hole, Bilbo Baggins was sure that there had been a mistake. The events of that evening changed Bilbo's life and set in motion events that transformed Middle-earth forever.

DWARVES

The bearded Dwarves were proud, secretive folk, who welcomed few visitors to their mountain halls. Dwarves were skilled at working with metal and stone and their underground cities were wondrous to see.

The Lost Kingdoms

In the Third Age, many of the Dwarves' cities were overrun by orcs, goblins and monsters. They had also been driven from the mines of the Grey Mountains and Moria, while the dragon Smaug had taken Erebor, the Lonely Mountain. The Dwarves wandered the world, planning to reclaim all that they had lost.

Gold, Steel and Mithril

The Dwarves crafted wonderful jewellery out of gold and forged magnificent swords made from steel. But the metal that they loved most was mithril. This precious metal was only found in the Mines of Moria.

Mithril chainmail was stronger than steel, but much lighter.

Thorin Oakenshield

Thorin's ancestors were Kings under the Mountain before the great dragon Smaug attacked. With his people killed or scattered, Thorin swore to take back his kingdom. Gandalf suggested that he needed a burglar, such as Bilbo Baggins, to sneak into Smaug's lair and spy out his weaknesses.

The Quest of Erebor

Thorin gathered twelve companions to help him to reclaim Erebor and its treasures. With Thorin as their leader, this was the company of thirteen dwarves who turned up at Bilbo Baggins's hobbit hole one fateful evening to invite him to join their quest.

Among the treasures Smaug had stolen was a great jewel called the Arkenstone.

BATTLE GEAR OF THE DWARVES

Being short and strong, dwarves used long-handled axes and war hammers in battle. The Dwarves fought long wars against the Orcs and Goblins. The tunnels and mines under the mountains rang with the clash of metal and the battle-cries of dwarves.

WAR HAMMER

LONG-HANDLED AXE

Mithril Helmet

Erebor — the Lonely Mountain

The Lonely Mountain had been one of the richest Dwarf-halls in Middle-earth. Now it was the lair of Smaug, a fiery dragon who slept on a pile of stolen treasure. It was here that Bilbo Baggins crept through a secret door to go and spy on Smaug.

MEN OF THE WEST

Once, the greatest of the kingdoms of Men had been Númenor. When it was lost under a great tidal wave, a handful of survivors escaped to found the kingdoms of the west: Arnor and Gondor.

The Rangers

Descendants of the kings of Arnor, the Rangers protected many lands from Sauron's evil, including the Shire. They called themselves Dúnedain, or 'Men of the West'. The Rangers were stern, grim-faced warriors and few people liked or trusted them. Yet they always held true to their ancient oaths to fight the Enemy.

Aragorn

Aragorn was the leader of the Rangers. He travelled widely through Middle-earth, from the icy wastes of the north to the southern deserts beyond Mordor. He was called Strider in the Shire, where many thought him a suspicious vagabond. But Strider came from a line of kings that stretched back to Númenor.

Aragorn would one day become King of Gondor, receiving the reforged sword of Isildur.

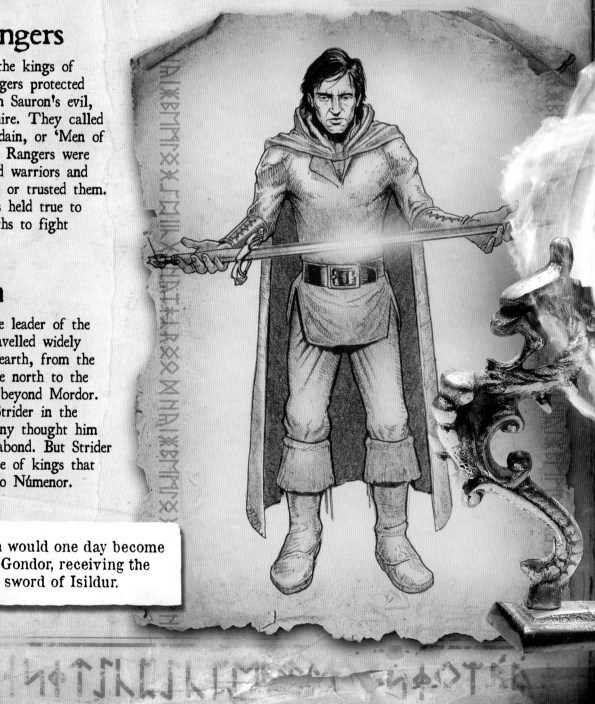

The Kingdom of Gondor

The warriors of Gondor protected the rest of Middle-earth from the armies of Sauron. From the walled city of Minas Tirith they watched over the bridges of the Great River. The last king of Gondor had been lost long ago and since then a line of Stewards had ruled in their place.

The Last Steward

Denethor II was the last Steward of Gondor. He dared to look into the Palantir of Minas Tirith. Its twin, the Ithil-Stone, had fallen into the hands of Sauron, but Denethor believed that he could wrestle control of this stone away from the Enemy. He failed, and Sauron drove him mad with terrible visions.

A Palantir could communicate with other Seeing Stones.

Heroes of the North

The Men of the North were not as long-lived or as wise as the descendants of Númenor, but they were always allies in the fight against Sauron. Most lived in Wilderland, between the Misty Mountains and Lake-town.

The Riders of Rohan

The Horse-Lords of Rohan lived on the green plains between the Misty Mountains and the Great River. Long ago they had ridden to help Gondor in battle and so the two peoples were firm friends.

During the War of the Ring, the wizard Saruman bewitched King Théoden with poison and lies. Just in time, Gandalf broke Saruman's enchantment, so that Théoden and his warriors could ride to battle against the armies of Sauron.

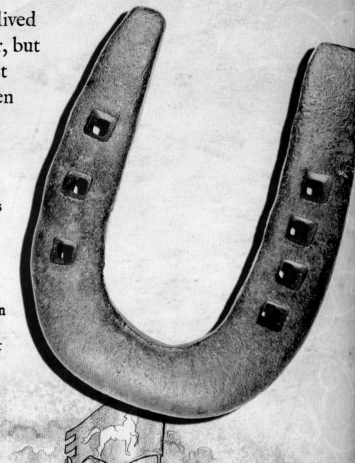

No enemy could withstand the charge of the Riders of Rohan.

Beorn

Beorn was a huge, bearded man who could turn himself into a bear. He lived alone on a farm in the middle of the wild lands. Beorn didn't like visitors, but he helped Bilbo and his companions during the Quest of Erebor and arrived to save them during the Battle of Five Armies.

The Fury of Smaug

Bilbo's theft of a golden cup angered Smaug, who took his revenge on Lake-town. Nothing could stop the dragon's fiery rampage, until a raven told Bard of Smaug's weak spot: a patch on his chest without scales or an armour-like layer of jewels.

ELVES

The Elves were the oldest and wisest of all the races. They were immortal and had lived in Middle-earth for thousands of years. Then, overwhelmed by sorrows, many had started to leave, sailing away to the Uttermost West. By the Third Age few remained.

Forest Realms

The Elves lived in the great forest realms of Mirkwood and Lothlórien, hidden from the gaze of Sauron and the other evil powers that hated them. In the Third Age, the largest Elf realms were Lothlórien, Rivendell, Mirkwood and the Grey Havens.

Elf Warriors

The Elves were the first to oppose the Enemy and they had fought against the Orcs and Goblins for thousands of years. Elf warriors were masters of swordplay, while an Elvish archer could bring down an orc from three hundred paces.

Legolas Greenleaf was a master archer and even brought down one of the Winged Nazgûl.

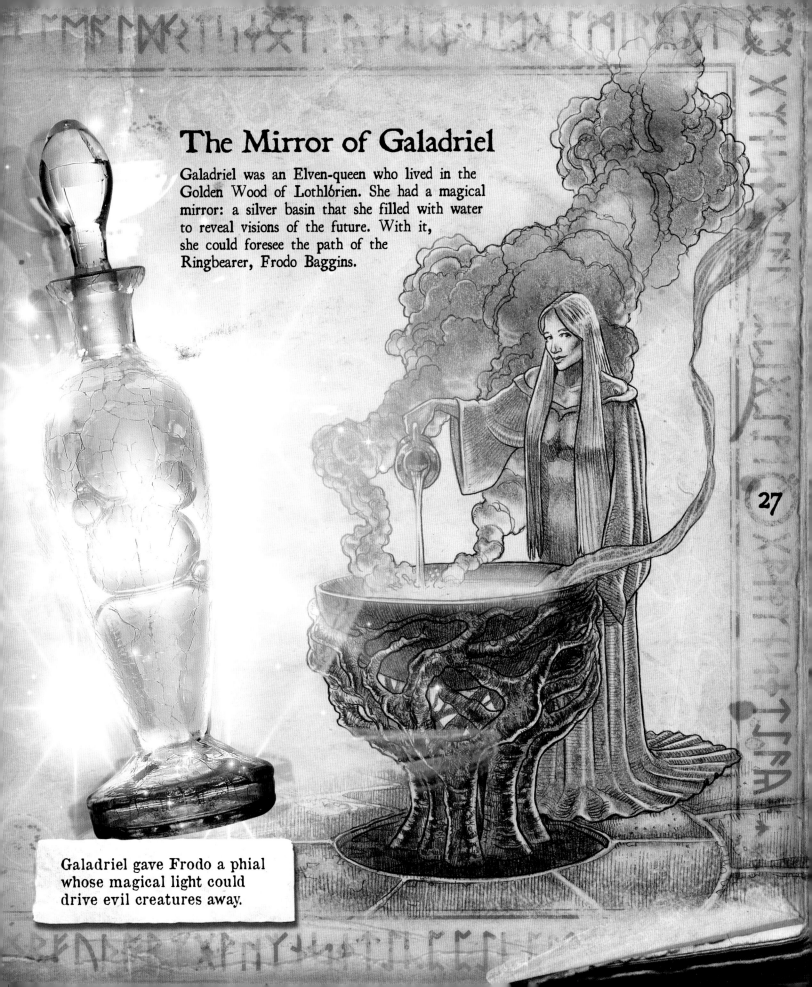

The Mirror of Galadriel

Galadriel was an Elven-queen who lived in the Golden Wood of Lothlórien. She had a magical mirror: a silver basin that she filled with water to reveal visions of the future. With it, she could foresee the path of the Ringbearer, Frodo Baggins.

Galadriel gave Frodo a phial whose magical light could drive evil creatures away.

RIVENDELL

The hidden valley of Rivendell was the magical, forested place where Elrond Halfelven lived. His house was one of the secret strongholds of the Elves.

Rivendell was also a refuge for the Dúnedain, men who were distantly related to Elrond on his human side. It was here that they kept the treasures of vanished Arnor: the Sceptre of Annúminas, the shards of the broken sword Narsil and the Ring of Barahir that was given as a token of friendship between Elves and Men in the Elder Days.

After his father Arathorn was slain by orcs, Aragorn was brought to Rivendell for protection. He grew up in Elrond's house and fell in love with his daughter Arwen. Elves are immortal, while Men are mortal, so those who were Half-elven had to choose whether to be Elves or mortals. If Arwen was to marry Aragorn, she had to become mortal and be forever parted from her father.

Arwen chose to marry Aragorn and she became the Queen of Gondor. In sorrow, Elrond left Rivendell for the Grey Havens.

It was in Rivendell that Aragorn met Arwen, his future wife and queen.

29

The Council of Elrond

The fate of Middle-earth was bound up in Bilbo's magic ring, the One Ring of Sauron. Frodo had carried it to the House of Elrond, where a council decided that Frodo and a Fellowship of eight companions would take the Ring to Mordor and destroy it.

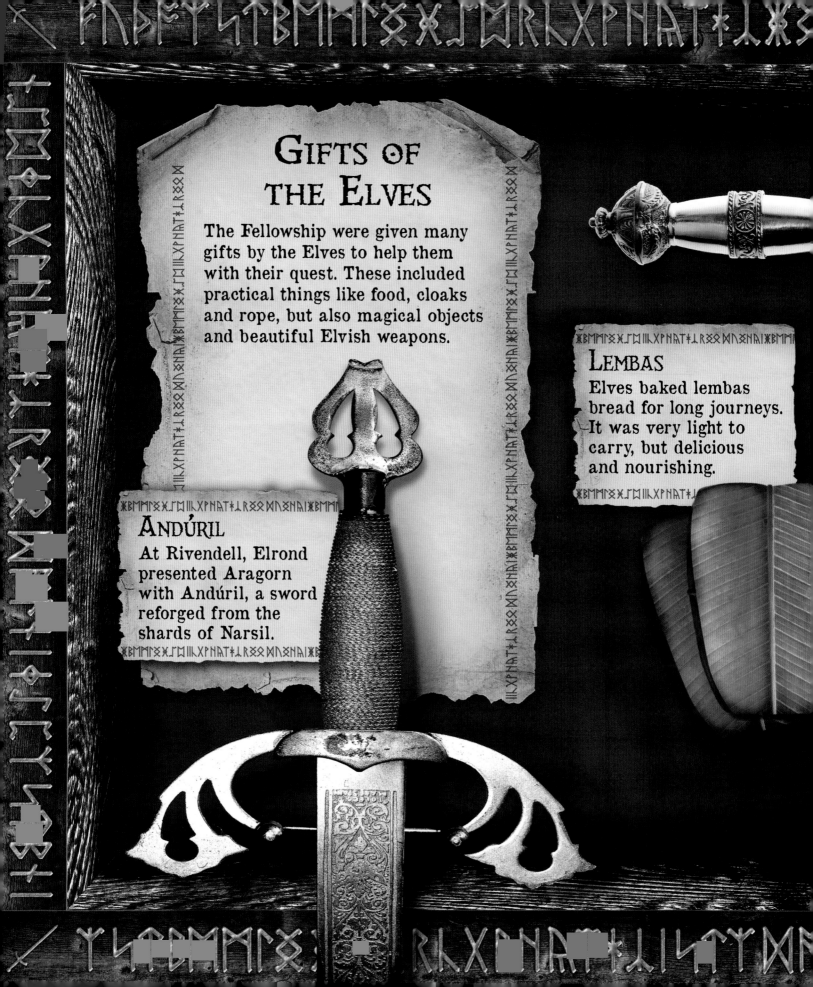

GIFTS OF THE ELVES

The Fellowship were given many gifts by the Elves to help them with their quest. These included practical things like food, cloaks and rope, but also magical objects and beautiful Elvish weapons.

LEMBAS

Elves baked lembas bread for long journeys. It was very light to carry, but delicious and nourishing.

ANDÚRIL

At Rivendell, Elrond presented Aragorn with Andúril, a sword reforged from the shards of Narsil.

ELVEN-DAGGER
Elven-smiths put magic spells on their best blades to make them glow when orcs were nearby.

BOW OF THE GALADHRIM
Galadriel gave Legolas a bow strung with a strand of Elf-hair.

GANDALF

Gandalf the Grey was one of five wizards sent to Middle-earth to defeat Sauron. The two Blue wizards vanished in the east, while Saruman the White and Radagast the Brown settled down to watch for the Enemy. Only Gandalf the Grey wandered the world.

The Wizards

Wizards looked like Men, but they were actually spirits sent by the Valar, the gods of Middle-earth. With their magical powers they held the evil of Sauron in check. Wizards were immortal. When Gandalf fell in battle against the Balrog, he was reborn as Gandalf the White.

Gandalf used his staff like a wand to create powerful magic.

Radagast

Radagast lived at Rhosgobel on the edge of Mirkwood. He was wise in the ways of nature and could speak the secret languages of birds and beasts. It was even said that he could turn himself into any animal.

Saruman

Saruman was the wisest of the wizards and their leader. He knew more of Sauron's secrets than anyone else, but this led him towards evil ambitions. He no longer dreamed of defeating Sauron, but of replacing him!

Gandalf took an interest in Hobbits and saw their hidden strength.

Forests of Middle-earth

Long ago, Middle-earth was covered in forests. The woods of the Third Age were huge, but they were just the remnants of a sea of trees that once spread far and wide. Elves lived in the forests, but evil things lurked there too.

The Old Forest

Just outside the Shire lay the Old Forest, where the paths moved and the trees whispered to each other. Hobbits sometimes ventured in by day, but never at night. Deep in the Old Forest was the house of an ancient nature spirit called Tom Bombadil.

Mirkwood

Mirkwood was a frightening place where the trees crowded together so tightly that it was always dark beneath their branches. A few elves still lived in Northern Mirkwood, but the rest of the forest was filled with spiders, vampire bats and monsters.

Lothlórien

The Golden Wood, Lothlórien, was home to Lady Galadriel and her High Elves. Few visited the forest, for men told stories of an enchantress who bewitched any travellers who ventured there. Lothlórien was protected by Galadriel's magic ring.

Tom Bombadil and his wife Goldberry were guardians of the Old Forest.

Treebeard was the
oldest of the Ents
and led them in the
attack on Isengard.

Fangorn Forest

Fangorn was the oldest and wildest forest of all
Middle-earth. Here, amidst the trees, lived the last
of the Ents, an ancient race of tree-like giants. Ents
were the tree-herders and forest-keepers of Fangorn
and guarded it against the axes of Saruman's orcs.

THE ENEMY

The Free Peoples lived under the shadow of evil. Rising once again from the land of Mordor was Sauron, the Dark Lord who wanted to conquer Middle-earth and make every living thing his slave.

Sauron's seat of power was the fortress of Barad-dûr, the Dark Tower he built with the power of the One Ring and which could not be destroyed while it existed.

The Orcs and Goblins were Sauron's soldiers, controlled by his will. But his armies also included wargs, vampires, dragons and trolls, while Barrow-wights and wraiths guarded the ways into Mordor.

Men also served Sauron, for the lands of the east had long been under his influence. Some worshipped him, others served him out of fear. Many served him out of greed, foolishly believing that they would be rewarded after the conquest of Middle-earth.

Sauron's chief servants were the nine Ringwraiths, or Nazgûl, who he controlled absolutely. Sauron held their Rings of Power, so they could never oppose him.

Not every evil thing in Middle-earth served Sauron. Some creatures, such as the giant spider Shelob and the Balrog, served their own dark purposes. Yet it was Sauron who was the one great Enemy of the Free Peoples.

SOLDIERS OF SAURON

Orcs and Goblins were the foot-soldiers of Sauron, but many races, including Men, were part of his vast armies. Alongside these soldiers, a host of other evil creatures served Sauron's evil will.

Orcs and Goblins

Orcs and goblins were cruel and savage. Many lived in the darkness under the Misty Mountains. Hating the light of the sun, they came out at night to make their attacks on the Free Peoples.

Many more orcs lived in Mordor in the shadow of Barad-dûr. The orcs of Mordor were bigger and stronger than the mountain goblins and their weapons were better made. They often used mountain goblins as scouts and trackers in their armies.

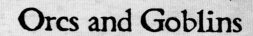

Uruk-hai

The Uruk-hai were a bigger and nastier kind of Orc. They stood taller than men and were stronger. Both Sauron and Saruman had Uruk-hai in their armies. They thought themselves better than the other orcs and bullied them.

Wargs

Evil spirits in the shape of wolves, wargs were clever and cunning. They lived in the valleys and forests along the River Anduin and united with the goblins to attack the Free Peoples. An army of wargs carrying goblins on their backs was a terrifying sight.

Orcs often smeared poison onto their blades to make them more deadly.

Orc War Gear

Weapons of Orc workmanship were brutally functional. Their war gear did not have the artistry of Elven-swords and weapons, but it was well-made and deadly.

Shield

Orcs carried heavy shields marked with the symbols of their masters, such as the red eye of Sauron or the white hand of Saruman.

Orc-Draught

Orcs drank a vile brew that restored strength and dulled pain to help them keep fighting.

Orc Helmet

As well as protection from sword or axe blows, orc helmets shielded their eyes from the hated sun.

Halberd

At the end of its long wooden handle, the halberd had a heavy, pointed blade.

SAURON

The great Enemy of Middle-earth, Sauron was an evil spirit from ancient times who wanted to rule all living things. He continued to weave wicked plots throughout the Second and Third Ages of Middle-earth.

At first, Sauron could take any shape he wished and could make himself seem charming and friendly. He used this power to trick the Númenóreans and bring about their destruction.

In the Second Age, Sauron tried to enslave all the Free Peoples of Middle-earth by forging a Ruling Ring. This would control all the Rings of Power worn by the leaders of the Free Peoples. But his plan failed and he lost the One Ring.

For many centuries, Sauron hid in Dol Guldur, the Hill of Sorcery. He slowly regained his strength and searched for the One Ring, which would give him the power to conquer all.

Gandalf discovered that Sauron was hiding in Dol Guldur and convinced the other Wizards to drive him out. But they were too late: Sauron had returned to his old fortress in Mordor and from there he commanded a vast army of Orcs, Goblins and monsters.

Sauron lost the Ring when his finger was cut off by Isildur on the slopes of Mount Doom.

Mordor — the Dark Tower

Sauron's stronghold lay in the land of Mordor, a terrible
place, surrounded by the Mountains of Shadow and the Dead
Marshes. Ash from Mount Doom rained down continuously
and orcs patrolled everywhere. Towering above a desolate
plain was the fortress of Barad-dûr, the Dark Tower from
where Sauron watched over all.

THE RINGS OF POWER

The Elves were the first to make rings with magic powers. A stranger called Annatar helped them to make rings for the leaders of the Free Peoples, but he was really Sauron in disguise. In secret, he forged the One Ring to control all the others and so rule Middle-earth.

THE ONE RING

Sauron forged the Ruling Ring in the fires of Mount Doom. He put all his power into it to bend the other rings to his will.

THE THREE RINGS OF THE ELVES

One ring was given to Galadriel. A second went to Elrond. The last ring, the Ring of Fire, passed into the hands of Gandalf.

THE SEVEN RINGS OF THE DWARVES

The Dwarves used their rings unwisely. Some were captured by Sauron, others were eaten by dragons.

THE NINE RINGS OF MEN

Nine rings were given to the kings of Men, who all fell under Sauron's power and became Ringwraiths.

Nazgûl

The deadliest of Sauron's servants were the nine Ringwraiths, or Nazgûl. Once, they had been the Kings of Men, but bewitched by Sauron they had become invisible wraiths.

Black Riders

Sauron sent the nine Nazgûl to search for the One Ring in the form of Black Riders. Their horses were ordinary horses, stolen from Rohan, but of the riders all that could be seen was their black hooded cloaks.

The Witch-king of Angmar

The leader of the Nazgûl was the Witch-king of Angmar. Second only to Sauron in evil, he had destroyed the kingdom of Arnor. In life, he had been a noble from Númenor, but as a wraith he was the the captain of Sauron's armies.

Morgul-knives

The Nazgûl carried knives forged in the city of Minas Morgul. If you were stabbed with one of these blades, a part of it could break off and then slowly work its way towards your heart.

A wound from a Morgul-knife could make its victim a wraith.

Winged Nazgûl

Mounted on monstrous flying beasts instead of horses, the Winged Nazgûl spread terror through the armies of the Free Peoples wherever they flew overhead.

51

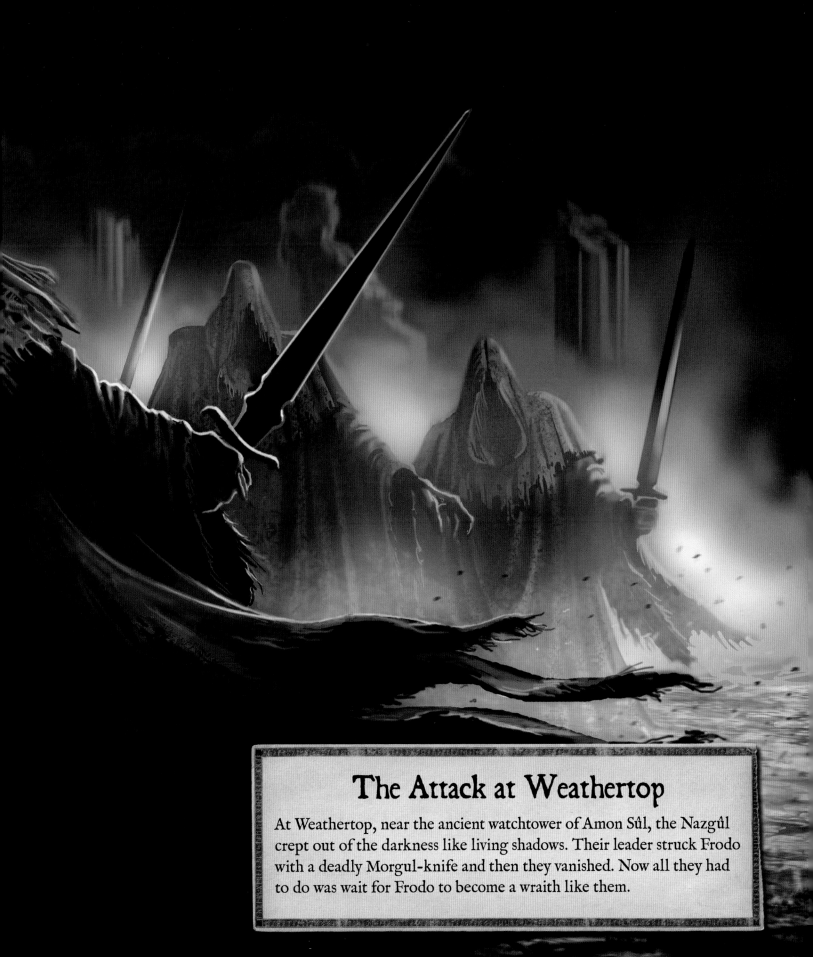

The Attack at Weathertop

At Weathertop, near the ancient watchtower of Amon Sûl, the Nazgûl crept out of the darkness like living shadows. Their leader struck Frodo with a deadly Morgul-knife and then they vanished. Now all they had to do was wait for Frodo to become a wraith like them.

The Fall of Isengard

The treachery of Saruman was a great blow to the Free Peoples. For many years he hid his evil ambitions from the other wizards and wove his plots from Isengard and the tower of Orthanc. Saruman planned to find the One Ring and take Sauron's place, but the Ents were his downfall.

LEGENDS AND LORE OF MIDDLE-EARTH

To become one of the Wise in Middle-earth, you had to learn all the books and rhymes of lore. Even among the Elves, few managed this feat and only those humans with very long lives, such as the Dúnedain, ever succeeded.

The greatest of the Wise formed the White Council. They watched for the movements of the Enemy and fought tirelessly against his evil.

Many tales, songs and legends make up the history and lore of Middle-earth. From the Elder Days to the end of the Third Age, the deeds of heroes and the knowledge of the Wise were kept alive by scholars and scribes.

One of the most important tales deals with the story of the Ruling Ring and how it was made and lost. For many centuries the whereabouts of the One Ring was a mystery to both the Wise and the Enemy. The unfolding of the story of the Ring is perhaps the greatest of the legends of Middle-earth.

Isildur and the Ring

Isildur cut the One Ring from Sauron's hand with the broken blade of Narsil, defeating the Dark Lord and winning the War of the Last Alliance at a single stroke. He had a chance to destroy the Ring, but Isildur kept it for himself.

The Scroll of Isildur

Before leaving for Arnor, Isildur wrote a scroll describing how the Ring had changed after he took it. The scroll was left in the library of Minas Tirith and there it lay, unread for three thousand years. Finally Gandalf found the scroll and discovered the secrets of the One Ring.

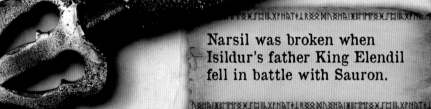

Narsil was broken when Isildur's father King Elendil fell in battle with Sauron.

The Gladden Fields

On his way north, Isildur and his men were ambushed by orcs at the Gladden Fields. They fought bravely, killing five orcs for every man that fell, but it was clear that the battle could not be won. Isildur's soldiers told him to escape while they held the orcs back. The young king ran and used the Ring's power of invisibility to hide from the orcs.

The Ring is Lost

The Ring was treacherous and at just the wrong moment it slipped off Isildur's finger. The orcs spotted him and Isildur died in a rain of arrows. The Ring was lost in the waters of the Gladden Fields and lay hidden from sight for many years.

SWORDS OF THE TROLL HOARD

When Bilbo and the dwarves were caught by trolls at the start of the Quest of Erebor, Gandalf saved them and the trolls were turned into stone. In the troll's lair they found treasure and three Elvish blades of ancient and magical craftsmanship.

ORCRIST

The sword taken by Thorin Oakenshield was named Orcrist, which means Goblin-Cleaver in the Elvish language of Sindarin.

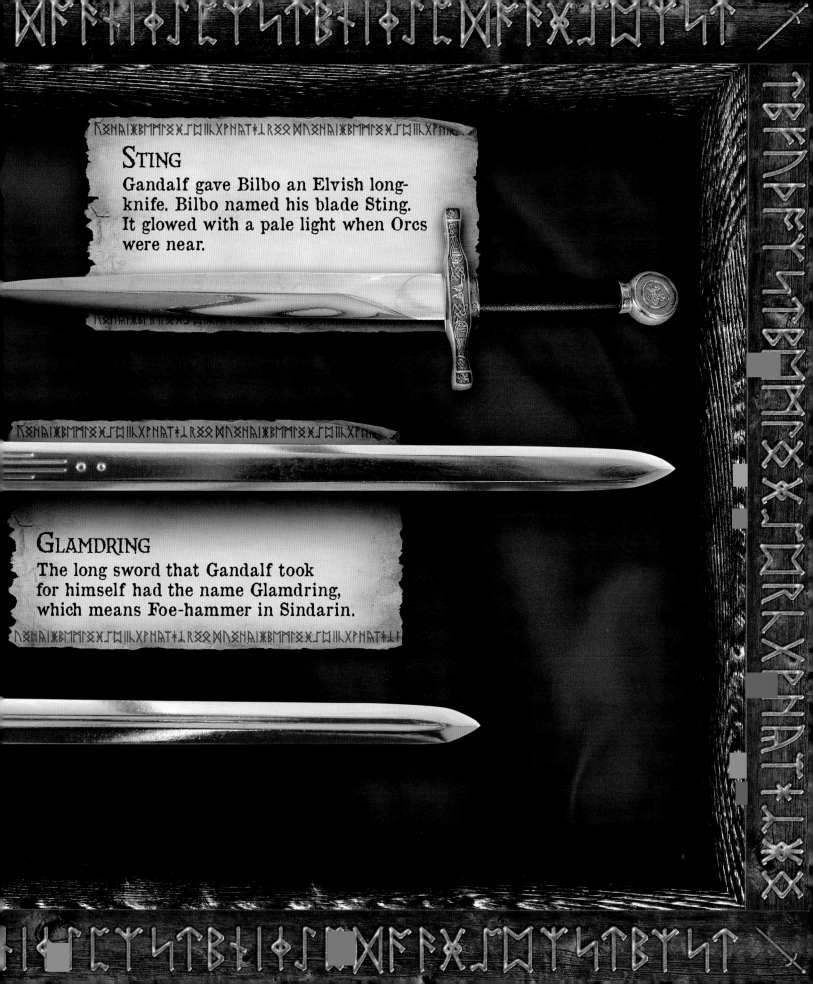

STING

Gandalf gave Bilbo an Elvish long-knife. Bilbo named his blade Sting. It glowed with a pale light when Orcs were near.

GLAMDRING

The long sword that Gandalf took for himself had the name Glamdring, which means Foe-hammer in Sindarin.

GOLLUM

Gollum was once a hobbit called Sméagol who lived on the banks of the Great River. His transformation from a hobbit to a hideous monster was due to the evil of the Ring.

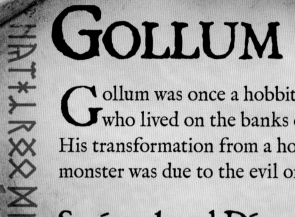

The Ring gave its bearer a long life, so Gollum looked very old.

Sméagol and Déagol

The Ring came into Sméaogol's hands when his friend Déagol found a shiny gold ring in the mud. Sméagol wanted it so much that he killed his friend and stole it. As time went by, Sméagol's mind was twisted by the Ring. Driven away by his family, he fled into the goblin caves under the Misty Mountains and hid in the darkness for centuries, slowly becoming the creature called Gollum.

The Precious

Gollum called the One Ring his 'Precious'. He used its power of invisibility to hide from the goblins, but Gollum never harnessed its full strength, which could conquer a world.

Riddles and the Ring

Gollum lost the Ring just before Bilbo got trapped in the goblin-caves. Bilbo picked up the Ring by chance and escaped with it after beating Gollum in a game of riddles. During the game, Gollum guessed that Bilbo had found his Precious and swore to get it back.

Gollum lived off raw fish and unlucky goblins who strayed into his clutches.

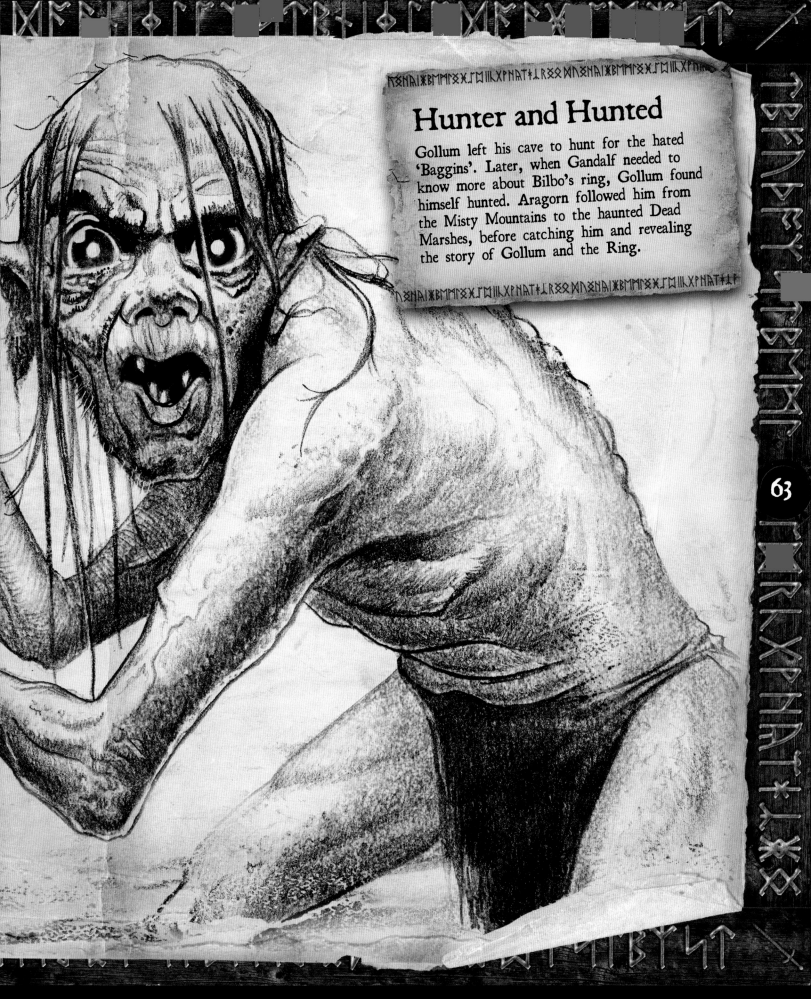

Hunter and Hunted

Gollum left his cave to hunt for the hated 'Baggins'. Later, when Gandalf needed to know more about Bilbo's ring, Gollum found himself hunted. Aragorn followed him from the Misty Mountains to the haunted Dead Marshes, before catching him and revealing the story of Gollum and the Ring.

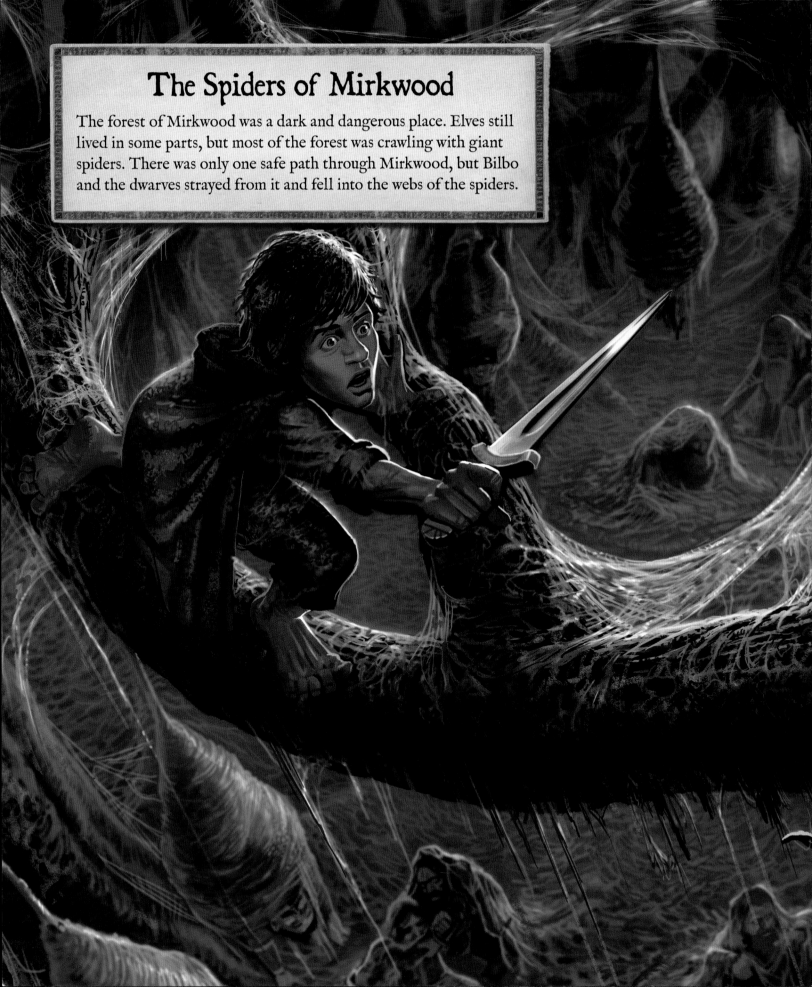

The Spiders of Mirkwood

The forest of Mirkwood was a dark and dangerous place. Elves still lived in some parts, but most of the forest was crawling with giant spiders. There was only one safe path through Mirkwood, but Bilbo and the dwarves strayed from it and fell into the webs of the spiders.

THE BATTLE OF FIVE ARMIES

After Bard killed Smaug, five armies clashed in the shadow of the Lonely Mountain. The Free Peoples triumphed, but at a great cost. Many lay dead, including Thorin Oakenshield, the uncrowned King under the Mountain.

THE FREE PEOPLES

DWARVES

SIZE OF ARMY: More than 500, including the twelve companions of Thorin Oakenshield.

ORIGIN: Most of the Dwarves marched from the Iron Hills, roughly 80km east of the Lonely Mountain.

WEAPONS: Two-handed axes, swords.

HEROES: Thorin Oakenshield, Dain Ironfoot.

MEN

SIZE OF ARMY: Probably less than 500.

ORIGIN: Lake-town and the villages south of the Desolation of the Dragon.

WEAPONS: Swords, bows, spears.

HEROES: Bard the Bowman, Beorn.

ELVES

SIZE OF ARMY: Around 1,500.

ORIGIN: The forest realm of Mirkwood

WEAPONS: Swords, spears, Elven-bows

HEROES: King Thranduil.

THE ENEMY

GOBLINS

SIZE OF ARMY: 10,000 or more.

ORIGIN: The Misty Mountains.

WEAPONS: Swords, daggers, spears, arrows, sharp-pointed teeth.

HEROES: Bolg, Son of Azog.

WARGS

SIZE OF ARMY: More than 5,000.

ORIGIN: The vales of Anduin.

WEAPONS: Claws and teeth.

HEROES: The Great Grey Wolf.

The eagles arrived at the height of the battle to help the Free Peoples defeat the Enemy.

THE QUEST OF THE RING

In Rivendell it was decided that the Ring should be taken to Mordor and destroyed. Frodo Baggins, a humble hobbit, bravely volunteered for this task, although he knew that there was little hope of success.

The Road to Mordor

The only way to stop Sauron was to destroy his Ruling Ring. That meant throwing it into the fires of Mount Doom in Mordor, the place where it had been forged. The road to Mordor would be a dangerous one for a small hobbit to take.

LEGOLAS GREENLEAF
An Elven-prince of the Woodland Realm in Mirkwood.

GIMLI
A Dwarven warrior from Erebor, the Lonely Mountain.

BOROMIR OF GONDOR
A mighty warrior and leader from the race of Men.

PEREGRIN TOOK
Known as Pippin. One of Frodo's Tookish cousins.

ᛘᚨᚠᛋᛖᛒᛁᛏᛟᛋᚲᚫᚠᚨᛋᛟᛁᛋᛏᛒᛁ

The Fellowship

Lord Elrond sent a band of companions with Frodo. Elrond had decided that there should be nine in the Fellowship, to oppose the nine Ringwraiths, and that the Fellowship should include all the Free Peoples: Men, Elves, Dwarves and Hobbits.

The Secret Quest

The armies of the Enemy were too powerful to defeat in battle. It was only by destroying the Ring that the Free Peoples could win. The Fellowship travelled in secret to avoid Sauron's spies. The fate of all Middle-earth rested with Frodo and his companions.

MERIADOC BRANDYBUCK

Known as Merry, one of Frodo's Buckland cousins.

FRODO BAGGINS

Nephew of Bilbo and the Ringbearer.

SAMWISE GAMGEE

Frodo's gardener and loyal friend.

STRIDER THE RANGER

Chieftain of the Rangers, but really Aragorn, heir to the throne of Gondor.

GANDALF THE GREY

Powerful wizard, known as The Grey Pilgrim.

FRODO BAGGINS

When Bilbo retired to Rivendell, he left everything that he owned to his nephew Frodo, including his magic ring. Gandalf kept an eye on the young hobbit, suspecting that the ring was the One Ring that Sauron had lost.

The Ring Revealed

Isildur's scroll had told Gandalf about some invisible letters written on the Ring, which would reappear if it was heated. Gandalf proved that Bilbo's ring was Sauron's Ruling Ring by throwing it into the fire at Bag End and revealing its magical inscription.

Frodo the Ringbearer

Following Gandalf's advice, Frodo took the Ring to Rivendell. To carry the Ring was a dangerous task. Even before he reached Elrond's House, Frodo had been attacked by the Nazgûl and wounded with a Morgul-knife.

Evil of the Ring

Frodo accepted the task of destroying the Ring and faced great hardships on the road to Mordor. But worse than all the wounds he suffered was the evil influence of the Ring. At times it came close to taking over his mind, as it had Gollum's.

Arwen gave Frodo a white jewel with the power to ease the pain of the Ring's loss.

The Adventure Ends

After his adventures, Frodo returned to the Shire, but he had suffered too much to return to normal hobbit life. Frodo finished writing Bilbo's story of the One Ring and then left Middle-earth, sailing across the sea from the Grey Havens.

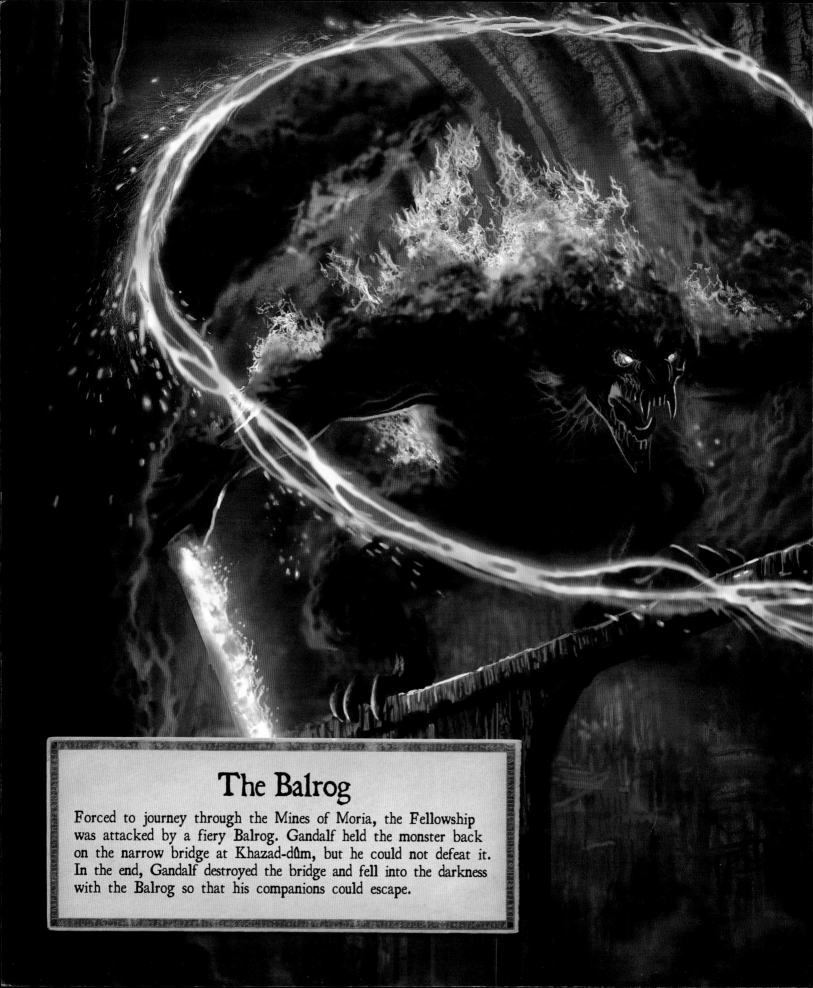

The Balrog

Forced to journey through the Mines of Moria, the Fellowship was attacked by a fiery Balrog. Gandalf held the monster back on the narrow bridge at Khazad-dûm, but he could not defeat it. In the end, Gandalf destroyed the bridge and fell into the darkness with the Balrog so that his companions could escape.

THE HORN OF GONDOR

Boromir carried the Horn of Gondor. A blast on the horn would summon help within the borders of Gondor, driving the servants of Sauron mad with fear. When Boromir fell in battle the horn was broken and was never heard again in Middle-earth.

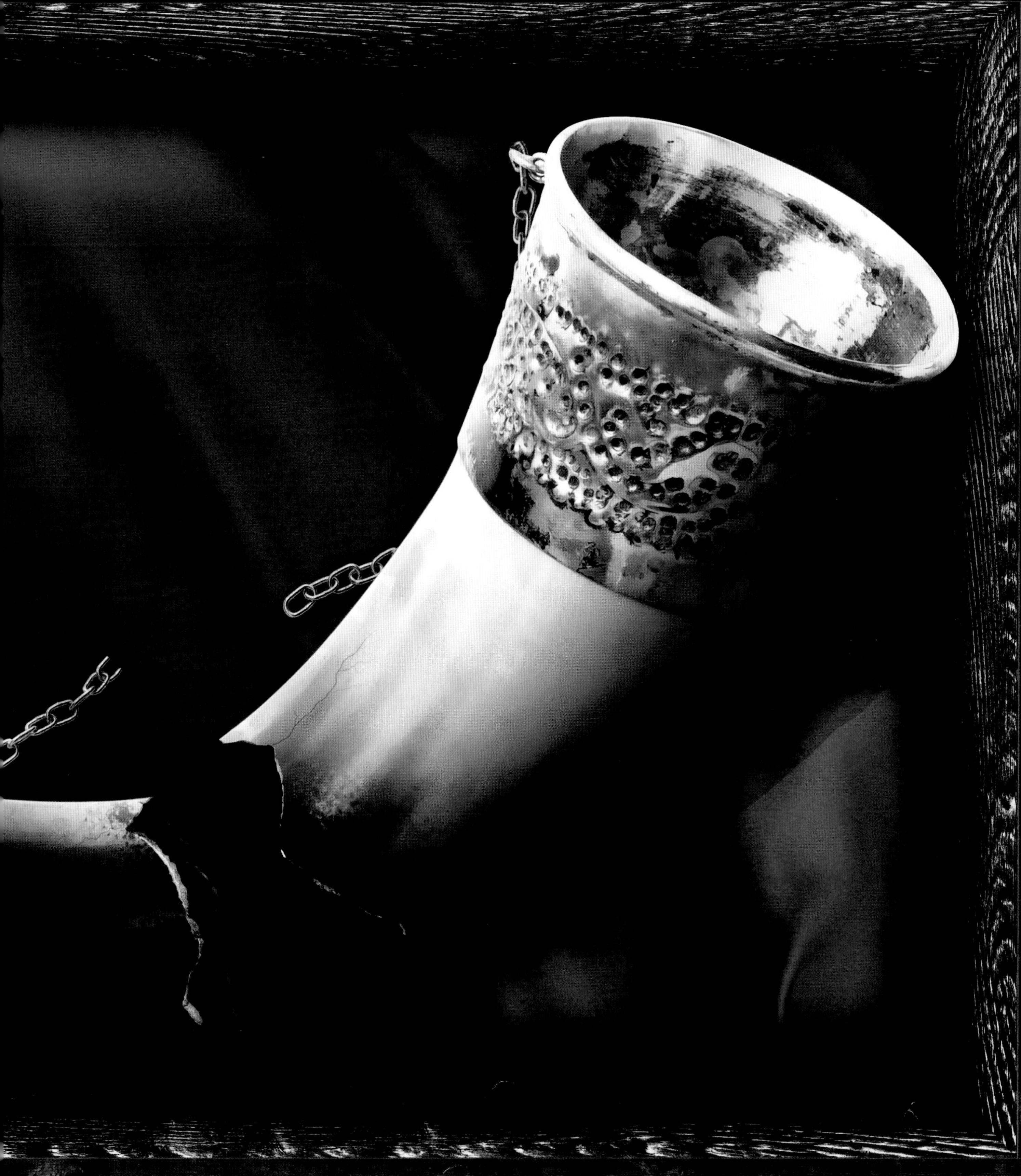

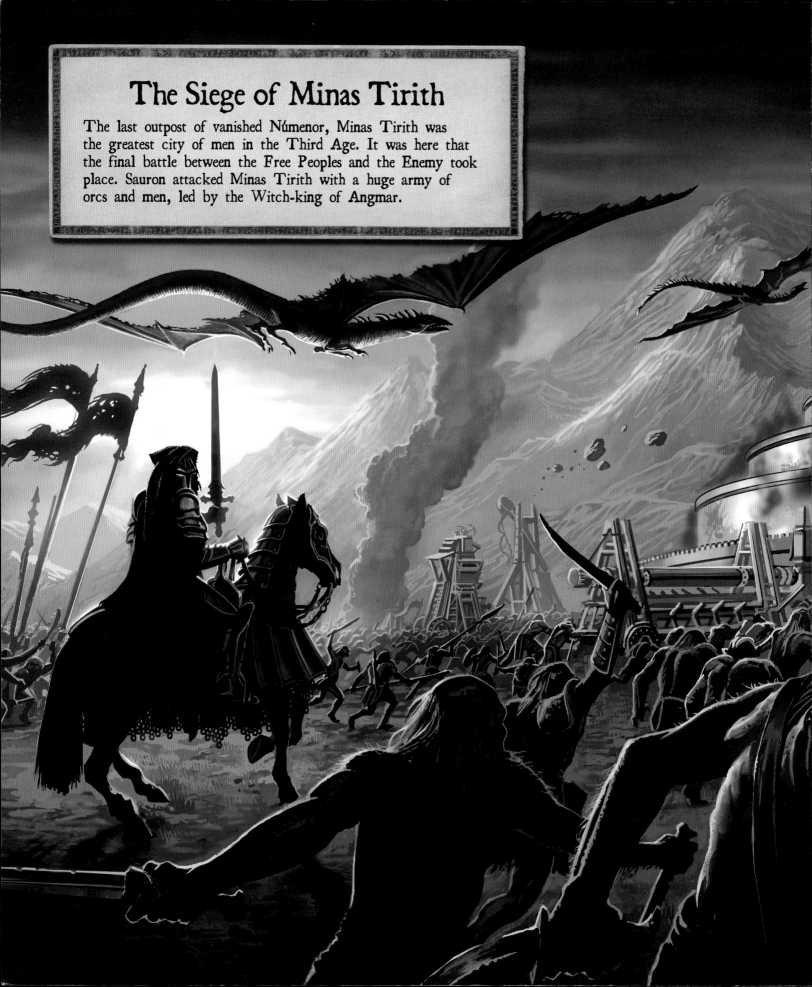

The Siege of Minas Tirith

The last outpost of vanished Númenor, Minas Tirith was the greatest city of men in the Third Age. It was here that the final battle between the Free Peoples and the Enemy took place. Sauron attacked Minas Tirith with a huge army of orcs and men, led by the Witch-king of Angmar.

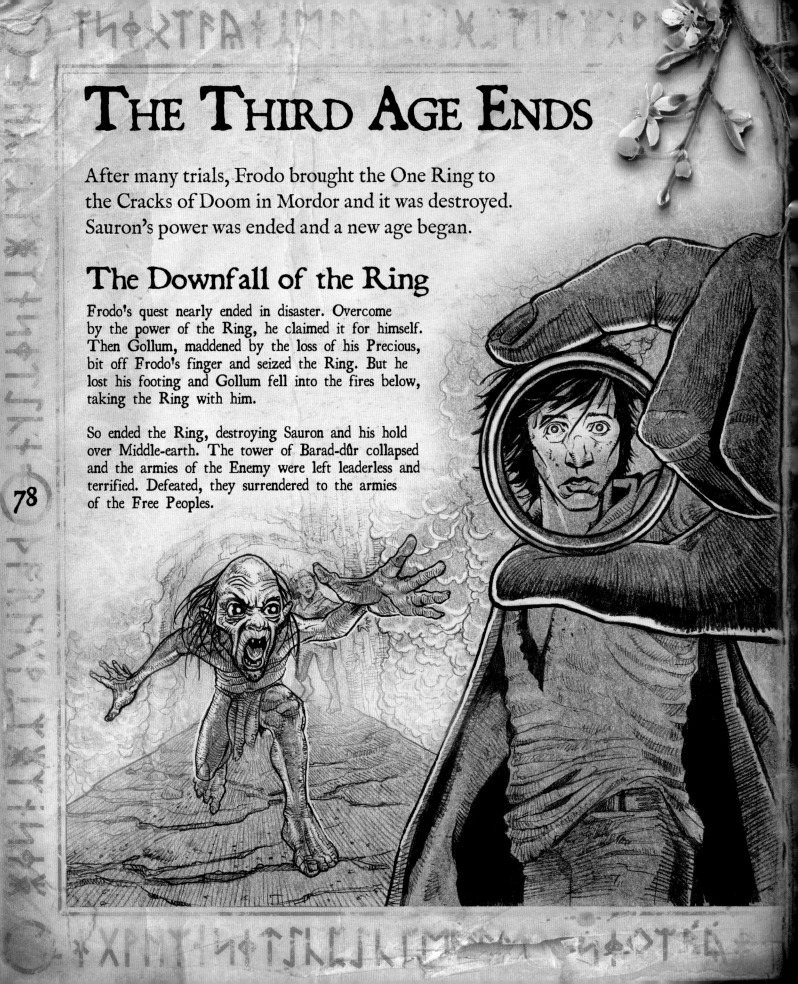

THE THIRD AGE ENDS

After many trials, Frodo brought the One Ring to the Cracks of Doom in Mordor and it was destroyed. Sauron's power was ended and a new age began.

The Downfall of the Ring

Frodo's quest nearly ended in disaster. Overcome by the power of the Ring, he claimed it for himself. Then Gollum, maddened by the loss of his Precious, bit off Frodo's finger and seized the Ring. But he lost his footing and Gollum fell into the fires below, taking the Ring with him.

So ended the Ring, destroying Sauron and his hold over Middle-earth. The tower of Barad-dûr collapsed and the armies of the Enemy were left leaderless and terrified. Defeated, they surrendered to the armies of the Free Peoples.

78

As a symbol of the rebirth of Gondor, Aragorn planted a sapling from ancient Númenor in the city of Minas Tirith.

The Return of the King

Aragorn arrived to save Minas Tirith when all had seemed lost. Following his victory, he claimed the throne of Gondor and the line of kings was restored. Aragorn made Arwen, the daughter of Elrond, his queen. She brought the blessings of the Elves to the renewed kingdom of Men.

The Grey Havens

With the fall of Sauron, the power of magic, both good and evil, faded away in Middle-earth. Many elves departed across the sea to the Undying Lands. With them went the wizard Gandalf and Bilbo and Frodo Baggins, the two hobbits who had been Ringbearers.

Acknowledgements

The author would like to thank the following for their invaluable assistance in the making of this book:

Firstly, my wonderful wife, Edel Ryder-Hanrahan, for her encouragement and for putting up with the late night emails and mutterings about elves; James Wallis for the timely introductions; Paul Virr for his steady editorial direction and insight; Jake da'Costa for his artistic guidance and Peter Mckinstry for his wonderful illustrations; Russell Porter and Luke Wijsveld for their fine design work; Ben White for his spot-on picture research; Mark Walker and Drew McGovern for their Photoshop magic and Claire Halligan for such superb production. Finally, my late mother Helen for introducing me to the magical world of Middle-earth all those years ago.

Picture Credits:

The publishers would like to thank the following sources for their kind permission to reproduce the pictures in this book.

Key, t: top, b: bottom, l: left, r: right.

Alamy: 60-61c, 60-61b, /color to go: 16; AKG Images: /Hermann Historica: 17l; Corbis: /Arte & Immagini srl: 42l; DK Images: 40-41, 41b; Getty Images: / Gary Ombler: 14-15, /Shun Sasabuchi: 27; iStockphoto.com: 14bl, 21, 32b, 48, 49t, 58; Royal Armouries: 42t; Stock.XCHNG: 51; Thinkstockphotos.com: 5, 15b, 17, 22, 32r, 33t, 41r, 48bl, 48br, 50, 61t, 62b, 71, 74-75, 79. All other photos and illustrations © Carlton Books Ltd.

Every effort has been made to acknowledge correctly and contact the source and/ or copyright holder of each picture and Carlton Books Limited apologizes for any unintentional errors or omissions, which will be corrected in future editions of this book.

This is a Carlton book.

Text, design and illustration © Carlton Books Limited 2013

Published in 2013 by Carlton Books Limited, an imprint of the Carlton Publishing Group, 20 Mortimer Street, London, W1T 3JW.

A catalogue record for this book is available from the British Library.

ISBN: 978-1-78312-049-9

Printed in China.